UNIVERSITY OF NORTH CAROLINA
Studies in the Romance Languages and Literatures

Number 30

PIERRE BAYLE
AND SPAIN

PIERRE BAYLE
AND SPAIN

BY

KENNETH R. SCHOLBERG

The Ohio State University

CHAPEL HILL
THE UNIVERSITY OF NORTH CAROLINA PRESS

Copyright, 1958, by
The University of North Carolina Press

Manufactured in the United States of America
Presses of The Orange Printshop, Chapel Hill, North Carolina

CONTENTS

Pierre Bayle and Spain   1

Appendices
   I.   Spanish and Portuguese Writers
          Referred to in the Works of Bayle   35
  II.   Translations of Hispanic Works
          Mentioned by Bayle   38

PIERRE BAYLE
AND SPAIN

PIERRE BAYLE AND SPAIN

ALTHOUGH MANY STUDIES exist on different aspects of Pierre Bayle's work—on his religious and philosophical ideas, his literary criticism, and his relation to French and English writers—little or nothing has appeared about his attitude toward Spain and his opinions of the writers of the Iberian Peninsula. The lack of interest in this segment of Bayle's thought is perhaps explicable. In some respects his work was extremely influential, for it was Bayle's scepticism which set the pattern for the Encyclopedists who came after him. Montesquieu and Voltaire and their associates looked on Spain as the land of Torquemada and the Inquisition, and largely because of them it became a commonplace in the eighteenth century to contrast the benefits of "la saine philosophie" with the horrors of the Inquisition. The French Romantic view of Spain inherited this conception. But Bayle's erudite interest in Spanish writers was not so widely followed, and in the Peninsula itself he was overshadowed by his successors. His influence on Feijóo has been noted by Américo Castro[1] and Paul Mérimée,[2] and his *Nouvelles de la République des Lettres* was one of the inspirations for the *Diario de los literatos*, founded in 1737. In their introduction the compilers of this early journal spoke glowingly of their French model: "Las *Noticias de la República de las letras* tuvieron principio en marzo de 1684 por el famoso Bayle, que depositó en ellas su admirable erudición y felicísimo ingenio." But it was to Voltaire, Diderot, and their contemporaries that the *afrancesados* of the eighteenth century turned, rather than to the author of the *Dictionnaire historique et critique*. In the modern period some peninsular critics may have been dissuaded from a consideration of Bayle by the overwhelming and utter condemnation of him by Menéndez y Pelayo, who called his *Dictionnaire* an

enorme *congéries* de toda la erudición menuda amontonada por dos siglos de incesante labor filológica: repertorio de extrañas curiosidades, aguzadas por el ingenio cáustico, vagabundo y maleante del autor, enamorado, no de la verdad,

---

[1] Américo Castro, "Algunos aspectos del siglo XVIII," *Lengua, enseñanza y literatura* (Madrid, 1924), p. 297.

[2] Paul Mérimée, *L'Influence française en Espagne au dix-huitième siècle*, Etudes Françaises, No. 38 (Paris, 1936), p. 89.

sino del trabajo que cuesta buscarla, y amigo de amontonar nubes, contradicciones, paradojas y semillas de duda, sobre todo en materias históricas.³

Of course, Menéndez y Palayo was an arch-conservative, especially in the early *Historia de los heterodoxos*. His own outlook was so at variance with that of Bayle that we could expect from him no sympathetic understanding of the attitudes and aims of the author of the *Dictionnaire*.

Nevertheless, Bayle's interest in Spain's history and in her literature merits consideration. His comments on the writers of the Iberian Peninsula form a not inconsiderable portion of his vast production. They are of interest because they reveal the ideas that were held and spread by this one person, outstanding for his influence on his contemporaries and on succeeding generations, and because they give us information about the extent and type of peninsular writings that were available in France and the Low Countries at the end of the seventeenth and beginning of the eighteenth centuries. His work should be recognized as an important source of material for those concerned with the exchange of ideas and culture between France and Spain.

Bayle's knowledge of Spain was gained almost entirely from literary sources and a few conversations with friends. He never travelled south of the Pyrenees; indeed, after his conversion to Catholicism and his subsequent relapse, such a voyage would have been impossible for him. He did, however, know the *Relation d'Espagne* of Mme. d'Aulnoy and the comments on Spain and Portugal of the Baron de Lahontan, both of whom he quoted to the detriment of the Spanish character (O.D. III, 1056, Réponse).⁴ Similarly he accepted at face value and repeated a somewhat scabrous story about Spanish monks and their *forfanteries* which had been related to him, he said, by the then deceased Frémont d'Ablancourt (D. VIII, 159, Hirpins, C). Unlike his situation *vis à vis* English literature, Bayle seems to have had

---

³ Marcelino Menéndez y Pelayo, *Historia de los heterodoxos españoles* (Santander, 1947), V, 13.

⁴ The following abbreviations are used throughout this article: The *Dictionnaire historique et critique* (16 vols., ed. Beuchot, Paris, Desoer, 1820), is referred to as "D." Besides volume and page, article and note are given except when the references are consecutive. *Oeuvres Diverses, contenant tout ce que cet auteur a publié ... . excepté son Dictionnaire ...* . (4 vols., La Haye, 1737), is referred to as "O.D." Where pertinent, the name and the date of the individual work are included. Spelling has been modernized in direct quotations.

almost no direct contact with Spaniards. The only mention of a Spanish correspondent I have been able to find is that of a certain Carrera, a Spaniard living in London who had written to Bayle and whom the latter mentions in a passage having nothing to do with Spain (O.D. I, 437, N.R.L., Dec. 1685). On the other hand, in his study of Spanish writers he had the advantage, which he did not have in relation to English,[5] of being able to understand the language. It is true that most of his sources for Spain were in French, Latin, and even Italian, but there are sufficient Spanish quotations or references to Spanish books read in the original to justify saying that he could read Spanish well enough for his needs. Among peninsular writers whom he used as sources, the two most important were Nicolás Antonio and Father Juan de Mariana, both of whom he read in Latin. A number of works were known by Bayle in their French translations, some of which he reviewed in the *Nouvelles de la République des Lettres*. Among these were *La semaine de Montalban, ou les mariages mal assortis ... . traduites de l'Espagnol par XX* (O.D. I, 381, N.R.L., Sept. 1685), *L'Homme de Cour, traduit de l'Espagnol de Baltasar Gracian, par le Sieur Amelot de la Houssaie* (O.D. I, 97, N.R.L., July 1684), and *L'histoire de la conquête de la Floride ... . écrite en Portugais par un Gentilhomme de la Ville d'Elvas et traduit en Français par M.D.C. (de la Guette de Citri)* (O.D. I, 295, N.R.L., May 1685). In the *Dictionnaire* the French translations that the author specifically states he used include the *Confusion de la secte de Mahumed* of Juan Andrés, translated by Guy le Fèvre de la Boderie (D. II, 86, André), Juan Huarte's *Anacrise ou parfait jugement et examen des esprits*, translated by Gabriel Chappuis (D. VIII, 292, Huarte, A), and Guevara's *Reveille-Matin des Courtisans*, translated by Alexandre Hardy, and his *Horloge des Princes*, translated by R. B. de Grise (D. VII, 326-27, Guevara, G and H). Occasionally Bayle resorted to an Italian translation of a Spanish work: he used the Italian version of Pedro Cieza de León's history of Peru (D. IX, 164, Leon, Pierre, A and B), and it is evident that he was familiar with Italian translations of Alfonso de Valdés' *Diálogo de Mercurio y Carón* and *Diálogo de Lactancio y un arcediano*, both attributed to Juan de Valdés (D. XIV,

---

[5] Bayle himself wrote (O.D. IV, 812, letter to M. des Maizeaux, Jan. 3, 1702): "Mon malheur est grand, de n'entendre pas l'Anglais, car il y a en cette langue beaucoup de Livres, qui me seraient très utiles."

309, Valdès, Jean de, E).[6] It may have been through preference that he used these translations, but he probably read them because they were more easily available than the originals.

As early as 1675, in a letter to his father, Bayle used the proverb "Ave muda non haze agüero" (O.D. I, 52) and in the *Pensées diverses,* his first important work, dating from March, 1682, he quoted a saying of the Conde de Villamediana about Philip IV (O.D. III, 28). In the *Continuation des pensées diverses* he gave Lope de Vega's well known poem on his method of writing plays, taken from the *Arte nuevo de hacer comedias* (O.D. III, 202). Sometimes his Spanish quotations were derived from a secondary source, as in the case of a passage about the siege of Pavia, which he took from Brantôme's *Capitaines étrangers* (D. XI, 327, Padilla, Jean de, D). Even more than in these occasional citations, we have definite proof of Bayle's knowledge of Spanish in his letter to M. Rou, dated February 21, 1696:

Vous ne savez pas, peut-être, qu'un certain Petrus Mantuanus publia en 1611 un Recueil en Espagnol des fautes de Mariana .... Un ami de Mariana nommé Tamaio, répondit à ce critique. J'ai lu le premier de ces deux ouvrages; jamais je n'ai pu trouver le second (O.D. IV, 723; see also D. X, 262, Mariana, C).

He also gives the impression of having known the Spanish translation, by Juan Vitrián, of the *Mémoires* of Philippe de Commynes (D. XI, 33, Naples, Alphonse 1er de, I). There can be no doubt that he read at least the introduction, by Jerónimo Serrano, to Juan de Espinosa's *Gynaecepaenos, o Diálogo en laude de las mugeres* in Spanish, for he quotes three long passages from it, one dealing with Espinosa's execution of justice in Italy, one on his book, the *Micracanthos,* and one about his collection of proverbs, which was not published and which Bayle says was lost. Of Espinosa's works he states: "Je n'ai vu que son *Gynaecepaenos* .... (D. XIII, 412 ff, Spinosa, Jean de, A and B). He also read the *Aviso sobre los abusos de la iglesia Romana* of the heretic Miguel de Montserrate in the original Spanish version. Besides repeating what Menéndez y Pelayo termed a "sañudo libelo .... de las monjas, que honradamente no puede transcribirse aquí,"[7] Bayle copied a passage dealing with the libidinous ardor of Spanish clerics, informing the reader that "je copie mot à mot jusqu'aux

---

[6] See Appendix II for a complete list of the translations of peninsular authors mentioned by Bayle.

[7] Menéndez y Pelayo, *Heterodoxos,* IV, 197.

fautes d'impression qui peuvent y être" (D. X, 490, Monserrat Montannes, A).

Bayle's literary sources of information on Spain were many and varied. Besides at least several hundred works of peninsular writers with which he was familiar, either in the original Spanish or Latin or in translation, he also used a number of secondary sources. To list all of them here would be pointless, but it is desirable to name those to which he referred most frequently. For historical matter Bayle used Mayerne Turquet's *Histoire d'Espagne*, the Abbé de Brantôme's *Capitaines étrangers*, Antoine de Varillas' history of heresies, Paul de Rapin's *Reflexions sur l'Histoire*, and the *Histoire Chronologique d'Espagne*, an *abrégé* based chiefly on Mariana, by a Mlle. XX (de la Roche), a Protestant refugee in Holland. Such were his major French sources. His Spanish sources included several historians of Charles V and Philip II, Luis de Avila y Zúñiga, the historian of the wars in Germany, the Conde de la Roca, Antonio de Herrera, et al. But first and foremost he relied on Juan de Mariana's *Historiae de Rebus Hispaniae* for his knowledge of Spanish historical figures, facts and interpretations. When his sources differed, he almost always gave preference to the great Jesuit historian.

Many of Bayle's Spanish comments and articles, especially in the *Dictionnaire*, dealt with theologians and religious writers, including a number of Spanish Protestants. This was a field in which he was particularly interested, and it is not surprising that he was familiar with the works of Luis de León, Molina, Melchor Cano, Juan de Valdés, and Martín del Río, to name but a few. His sources also included the *Bibliotheca scriptorum Societatis Jesu*, the *Mercure Jésuitique*, and, of course, the *Index* of prohibited books. For knowledge of Spanish literature he had at hand the *Bibliothèque française* of Du Verdier Vau-Privas, the *Hispaniae Bibliothecae* of Andreas Schottus, Baillet's *Jugement des Savants sur les principaux ouvrages des auteurs*, and, above all, the *Bibliotheca vetus* and *Bibliotheca nova* of Nicolás Antonio. It was to Baillet that Bayle probably owed whatever knowledge he had of such great literary figures of Spain and Portugal as Juan de Mena, the *Celestina*, Góngora, and Camões. As a matter of fact, purely creative literature—the novel, poetry, and the drama—held little interest for Bayle. In all of his works we find the name of Cervantes only in one footnote, telling that Audiguier had translated his *Novelas* (D. II, 52, Audiguier, N. d', A). Nicolás Antonio was undoubtedly the compiler to whom

Bayle turned most frequently for his facts on Spanish writers. We shall discuss his importance to the *Dictionnaire* later. Suffice it here to say that there are at least seven entries based entirely on Antonio, and there is rarely an article on a Spanish writer in which the name of Antonio does not figure.

Before we consider Bayle's opinions of Spain's writers, it might be well to discuss his attitude toward the Spanish nation and people as a whole. His instinctive, what one might term his unthinking, reaction to Spain was not favorable. Although he was an apostle of tolerance, or perhaps because he was an apostle of tolerance, his remarks about the Spanish character were not kind. He presents a rather stereotyped portrait of the Spaniards: they are great lovers, fond of vengeance, given to dueling and murdering their enemies, very superstitious and implacable toward heretics. His quotations from Mme. d'Aulnoy and from the Baron de Lahontan, mentioned previously, are of precisely those passages which present these aspects of the Iberians (O.D. III, 1056, Réponse). Elsewhere he mentions that the Spaniards are much addicted to gambling (O.D. I, 726, N.R.L., Jan. 1687). Furthermore, the savant of Rotterdam was unbelievably credulous in accepting and repeating tales attacking the abuses of Spanish monks. He did not hesitate to present as factual a story about a certain monastery

<blockquote>
qui fournit toutes les années un moine qui s'enferme dans un four chaud, et se tient là quelques heures habillé de simple toile. Il en sort à la vue d'une multitude de gens qui prennent cela pour un grand miracle. Cette affaire apporte un bon revenu à ce couvent, et vaut bien la peine d'accoutumer peu à peu un religieux à supporter la chaleur. Je ne compte pas tous les artifices qui peuvent entrer là dedans (D. VIII, 159, Hirpins, C).
</blockquote>

This particular story he had heard from his late friend Frémont d'Ablancourt, who he admits was a zealous Huguenot. He claimed that Ablancourt had named the location of the monastery, but that he had forgotten it. He also repeated the attacks on the Spanish clergy of Miguel de Montserrate, hardly a reliable source (D. X, 490, Monserrat, A). Bayle's purpose in using these libels was two-fold: in the first place he liked to enliven his work with such scandalous details, and, more important, they helped to destroy the authority of accepted religion and to induce a sceptical attitude toward all dogmatic belief, which was his primary aim.

Of course, Spain was for Bayle the land of the hated Inquisition and of intolerance. In the *Nouvelles de la République des*

Lettres of March, 1684, he expressed ironical amazement that the *Antoniana Margarita* of Gómez Pereira (who denied that animals have feeling) could have been produced "dans le pays du monde où l'on aurait le moins soupçonné qu'une doctrine si nouvelle prendrait naissance ... . Qui aurait jamais deviné que l'Espagne, où la liberté des opinions est moins soufferte que celle du corps ne l'est en Turquie produirait un philosophe assez téméraire pour soutenir que les animaux ne sentent pas ... .?" (O.D. I, 7). Two years later, in his *Commentaire Philosophique sur ces paroles de Jésus-Christ: Contrains-les d'entrer*, he scoffed at those French writers (that is, Catholic writers) who had reproached the Spaniards because of the Inquisition and who claimed greater merit for France in their methods of combating Protestantism. Bayle hoped, he said, to live long enough to see some able Spaniard prove the absurdity of their claims and to show them that their objections to the Inquisition arose only because they had not established it themselves. Then, in one of the most personal and bitter passages in his work, understandable in view of the tragedy which had recently befallen his older brother, he summarized with damning logic the consequences of a belief in forced conversion:

La vérité est qu'à la réserve de quelques procédures dans l'instruction des procès, lesquelles ne sont pas dans l'ordre, rien ne peut être plus lié avec le sens littéral des paroles *contrains-les d'entrer* que l'Inquisition; rien ne peut être plus juste ni plus louable que de faire mourir les Hérétiques comme font les Espagnols, posant une fois que Jésus-Christ commande de forcer d'entrer. Quelle horreur qu'il y ait un dogme parmi les Chrétiens, lequel une fois posé, il s'ensuit que l'Inquisition est le plus saint établissement qui ait jamais été sur la terre (O.D. II, 404).

It must be said to Bayle's credit, however, that he did not accept every aspect of the "Black Legend" of Spain. In his discussion of Pedro Cieza de León's history of Peru he took issue with those writers who would blame Europeans, and especially Spaniards, for having corrupted the pure and simple aborigines of America. He quoted a number of passages (in Italian) from Cieza de León's work to show the depravity of the natives, and went so far as to state that the most debauched of Spaniards could never have seen in their own country the abominations that they encountered in the New World (D. IX, 164 ff, León, Pierre Cieça de). Bayle could, upon occasion, see that the Spanish had been unjustly maligned. The fact remains, however, that he himself was not so impartial in treating their character as one might hope and even expect from a person of his vast erudition, but the age and atmosphere in which he lived must be taken into account before we judge him too harshly.

On a more scholarly level than these purely personal reactions to the Spaniards is his consideration of the causes for the antipathy that existed between the French and Spanish nations. This was a theme that he developed on several occasions, in the *Nouvelles de la République des Lettres*, the *Réponse aux Questions d'un Provincial*, and in the *Dictionnaire*. That such antipathy existed was accepted as a basic fact, reasonably so in view of contemporary French-Spanish relations. Bayle did not agree with all the reasons adduced to explain their rivalry, however. He refuted Varillas, who derived their mutual hatred from the time of Henry IV of Castile and Louis XI of France. In his *Histoire de Louis XI*, Varillas wrote that on the occasion of an interview between the two monarchs, the French king appeared so poorly dressed that the Spanish conceived instant scorn for the French and seized the first opportunity to break with them, and that the antipathy had continued from that time. Bayle considered this an extremely weak explanation (D. IX, 425, Louis XI, X; O.D. III, 522, Réponse). He reported the theory that the introduction of the House of Austria into Spain was the cause of friction, but pointed out that the French and Spanish were already embittered toward one another before Charles V came to the throne (O.D. I, 600, N.R.L., July 1686). Although in the *Nouvelles* he accepted La Mothe le Vayer's view, expressed in the *Discours de la contrariété d'humeurs qui se trouve entre de certaines nations*, that their opposition included not only political interests but also unimportant customs and "les humeurs des particuliers" (ibid.), his more sustained judgment was that it was really due to the struggle for power between the two nations. The Kingdom of Naples was an apple of discord between the kings of France and Aragon and the marriage of Marie de Bourgogne to Archduke Maximilian had exacerbated feelings between France and the House of Austria, but the real and basic cause was the unification of the kingdoms of Spain: "La Castille, l'Aragon et plusieurs autres états d'Espagne se réunirent: voilà l'origine de la haine des Français et des Espagnols; car depuis cette réunion la France a été toujours obligée ou de repousser l'Espagne ou de l'attaquer" (D. IX, 425, Louis XI). Antipathy to Spain was especially rampant during the religious wars of the sixteenth century. Bayle accused Philip II of being the evil genius of Catherine de'Medici and the spirit that animated the *Ligue*. Spanish influence reached its zenith then, and he claimed that France was not completely *desespagnolisée* until after the deaths of all those who had taken part in the *Ligue*. But at the same time that some of the people were so inclined toward Spain, others redoubled their hatred for her. The marriage of Louis XIII to Anne of Austria, daughter of Philip III, brought about an era of better relations, Bayle said, pointing out that it was in connection with this royal marriage that Doctor Carlos García composed his work on the *Antipatía de los franceses y españoles,* and noting that La Mothe le Vayer took many of his ideas from the Spaniard, although the latter was "incomparablement plus civile et plus honnête envers la France que La Mothe le Vayer envers l'Espagne" (O.D. III, 522-23, Réponse). In Bayle's own time, the wars of Louis XIV and Spain over Flanders, the Franche-Comté, and finally the War of the Spanish Succession, which Bayle did not live to see concluded, continued the antipathy. Even while these wars were being waged, Bayle could write:

J'oserais bien vous assurer que toutes ces antipathies dont on met la cause dans la diversité des tempéraments et des coutumes, et que sous ce prétexte-là on voudrait faire passer pour incurables, sont des chimères. Laissez à des nations voisines la différence de moeurs et d'usage, ôtez-leur la jalousie et l'affectation ou d'égalité ou de supériorité, et faites que les mêmes intérêts d'Etat les regardent, vous les verrez sympathiser en peu de temps et charier bien ensemble .... (O.D. III, 523, Réponse).

Bayle gives historical perspective to the relative positions of France and Spain. Developing a theme of Mariana's on the changes of Fortune, he remarked on the ascendancy and superiority of Spain in the fifteenth and sixteenth centuries, an ascendancy which must, in Bayle's opinion, give confusion to the French and pride to the Spanish. But the next century brought a change. The seventeenth century witnessed the downfall of Spain and the rise of France (D. XI, 27-28, Naples, Alphonse 1er de). Bayle pointed out the deep suspicion that was aroused in other European countries by the actions of the Spanish branch of the House of Austria. The events in the Low Countries, the part played by Spain in the civil wars in France, the invasion of Portugal, and the Invincible Armada were the reasons why people thought Spain aspired to universal monarchy and why "on s'était fait une idée affreuse de la politique d'Espagne." He himself wished to appear cautious about the charge:

Si j'ai dit, ou si je dis quelque fois dans la suite, que l'Espagne était accusée d'aspirer à la Monarchie Universelle, il ne faut pas croire pour cela que je prétende que cela fut vrai. J'agis en cela comme simple Historien, qui rapporte les bruits communs, sans se rendre garant de leur certitude. Ainsi je n'ai pas lieu de craindre d'irriter les Espagnols (O.D. IV, 908, Discours historique sur la vie de Gustave Adolphe).

Such delicacy about wounding the feelings of the Spanish is not found very frequently in Bayle's works.

Even if Spain's rulers had desired to rule the world, he concluded that there was little chance that they would have succeeded. Their slowness and long deliberations made them lose too many opportunities and because of weighing and re-weighing the same point a thousand times, it was impossible for them to carry out the conquests to which they were accused of aspiring (O.D. III, 146, Pensées diverses). All this, of course, was history. Now—that is to say, in Bayle's time—the Spanish were the first to clamor against those (i.e. Louis XIV) who would expand at the expense of their neighbors, and they were the most vociferous in wanting everyone to take up arms against such ambitious princes (O.D. IV, 908, Discours.... de Gustave Adolphe). In short, Spain was no longer the great power that she had been.

Bayle's interest in Spanish history, with the exception of the outstanding figure of Alfonso X, to whom he devoted much space, was limited almost entirely to Spain from the time of Charles V. He mentions earlier rulers, Alfonso V and Ferdinand of Aragon, Alfonso I of Naples, Urraca, daughter of Alfonso VI, Pedro *el cruel* and María de Padilla, Enrique III, and others, but his main concern is with the House of Austria. Charles V, he admits, was a great figure, the greatest produced by the House of Austria. But, he asks, what did he achieve? The wars he carried on for his religion were concluded to the advantage of the Protestants, and instead of conquering lands from France, he was not even able to recover from the French crown what it had previously seized. The emperor did have some attractive personal qualities. His knowledge of languages, his generosity toward Francis I, and, of course, some question as to whether he died in strictest Catholicism made him an interesting person for Bayle (D. V, 63 ff, Charles-Quint). Philip II was passionately hated by the author of the *Dictionnaire*. Besides accusing him of concerting the St. Bartholomew's Day Massacre with Catherine de' Medici at the interview of Bayonne and of being the motivating force behind the *Ligue*, which "ne se remuait que par les inspirations que les courriers lui apportaient de Madrid" (O.D. III, 522-23, Réponse), he says that "Philippe Second .... avait tellement accoutumé ses sujets à donner un tour de religion à toutes les affairs d'état qu'ils appellaient hérétique tout ce qui était contraire à l'Espagne, et Catholique tout se qui lui était favorable" (O.D. II, 184, Nouvelles Lettres Critiques). Of course, he does not fail to mention Philip's supposed ingratitude to his father (D. V, 72, Charles-Quint, O) or the tragic death of his son, don Carlos, obviously accepting the version that Philip had don Carlos put to death (O.D. III, 28, Pensées diverses).

The treatment accorded Alfonso X of Castile is especially interesting, not only because of the multitude of facts compiled about that monarch, but because of the insight that the article gives us about Bayle's method and purpose. His basic source was Mariana and he follows the Jesuit's judgments closely, although with important exceptions. He agrees with Mariana that Alfonso was a better scholar than a king. In fact, "..... il serait à souhaiter pour l'honneur des sciences qu'un prince qui en était si orné, eût conduit ses peuples avec plus de bonheur et plus de sagesse" (D. IV, 562, Castille, Alphonse X de). He also follows his Spanish source in saying that Alfonso lost the Empire because of his astronomical interests, quoting the famous "dumque coelum considerat observatque astra, terram amisit" (ibid., 564, G), and he accepts Mariana's harsh judgment that Alfonso was not loved by his own people or by his neighbors, and that his reputation improved with distance, but does not agree with the Spaniard on the consequences of Alfonso's use of the vernacular for his public documents. Mariana, it will be remembered, attributed to Alfonso's neglect of Latin "una profunda ignorancia de letras que se apoderó de nuestra gente y nación, así bien eclesiásticos como seglares."[8] Bayle does not accept this theory. He compares the situation in Spain with that in France and concludes that ignorance and barbarism were just as widespread in the latter country, even though a French regulation favoring the use of the vernacular was not established until the time of Francis I. In fact, the study of Latin in France was never more popular than after it was decreed that public acts were to be written in French (D. IV, 563-64, Castille, Alphonse X de, E).

Alfonso's life afforded Bayle's genius ample opportunity for changes of tone. In discussing the difficulties of the king's mar-

[8] Juan de Mariana, *Historia de España*, I, *Biblioteca de Autores Españoles*, 30 (Madrid, 1864), 412.

riage and Violante's early lack of an heir, he followed the generally accepted facts, but presented them in an amusingly flippant manner:

> La reine passa d'une extrémité à l'autre: elle eut neuf enfants; c'était plus qu'il n'en fallait pour le bonheur et pour le repos de son mari: ce fut pour ses péchés qu'il eut une femme si féconde. Encore ne se contenta-t-il pas de cette fécondité; il fit ailleurs quelques enfants à la dérobée (ibid., 560).

The fact that Alfonso received from the Pope certain rights to Church revenues in exchange for relinquishing his claims to the Empire gave Bayle the chance to include an anti-clerical note: "Il n'y eut que le clergé qui en souffrit; or il a de bonnes épaules; il ne faut pas le plaindre" (ibid., 563, B). The rebellion of Sancho allowed him to moralize on the evils of lust for power, although he admits that his moralizing is taken from Mariana (ibid., 562 and 567, M). Of Alfonso's literary work Bayle listed his translation of the Bible into Spanish, his legal work, the *Siete Partidas* (although he does not mention it by name), and the astronomical tables; he also grants that the Castilian king understood astronomy, philosophy, and history, and that he wrote books on the history of his country that are "très beaux" (ibid., 564, G and 566, K). Of greatest interest to Bayle were Alfonso's astronomical works, not because of their scientific content but because of their cost and because of the statement on the creation of the universe that was attributed to Alfonso. Although the actual cost of the *Tablas alfonsíes* was reckoned at four hundred thousand ducats (Bayle disagrees with Vossius, *De Scientiis Mathematicis*, who put the amount at *quadraginta ducatorum millia*), the real cost was that they made him lose the Empire (ibid., 564, G). Bayle appears sceptical about Alfonso's supposed statement to the effect that if the Lord had asked him for his advice at the time of creation, things would have been different. Listing a number of writers who repeated this story—Justus Lipsus, le père Théophile Raynaud, le père l'Enfant (who used Rodrigo Sánchez de Arévalo), and a Lutheran minister, Spizelius (Gottlieb Spizel), author of the *Felix Litteratus* — Bayle rejects all of them, relying on Mariana, who mentioned that Alfonso had dared to criticize the works of Providence but who admitted that this was only a popular tradition and that there was no contemporary account of the king's supposed irreverence. Although Bayle relates the longer version by Sánchez de Arévalo, repeated by l'Enfant, about the visions of a retainer of the Infante Manuel, those of a hermit of Segovia, and the terrible lightning storm that caused Alfonso to repent and confess his sins, he denies that it has any validity, because Mariana, who wrote after Sánchez de Arévalo and who was "infiniment plus habile et plus judicieux que lui," would not have suppressed these details, were they true (ibid., 565, H). Also relying on Mariana, he shows the error of Spizelius, who wrote that Alfonso died in exile (ibid.). Although he clearly rejects the story of the supposed blasphemy of the Castilian king, he feels that Alfonso would have been justified in uttering it. Following the lead of Fontenelle's *Pluralité des mondes*, he develops the argument that

si Alphonse porta sa critique sur quelque partie de l'univers, ce fut sur les sphères célestes. Car outre qu'il n'étudia rien tant que cela, il est sûr que les astronomes expliquaient alors le mouvement des cieux par des hypothèses si embarrassées et si confuses qu'elles ne faisaient point d'honneur à Dieu et ne répondaient nullement à l'idée d'un habile ouvrier (ibid.).

Bayle wrote in his review of the *Pluralité des mondes*, and repeated in the *Dictionnaire*, that if one changed Alfonso's supposed words to read "Que si Dieu avait fait le monde tel qu'on le suppose dans le système de Ptolémée, on pourrait lui donner de bons avis pour une autre fois," his scandalous daring would be greatly diminished (O.D. I, 548, N.R.L., May 1686; D. IV, 565, Castille, Alphonse X de, H). Thus, although Bayle rejected the canard about Alfonso, by repeating and discussing it he had the opportunity to spread further the modern ideas on astronomy being popularized by Fontenelle.

As for Alfonso's literary achievements, and particularly his rôle in compiling the laws of Spain, Bayle took the view that he merely ordered the works written and did not credit him with any personal contribution to their creation. He compared Alfonso to Theodosius, Justinian, and Louis XIV in that they caused to be written the codes which bear their names but did not actually compile them. In this he disagreed with Ridderus, *De Eruditione historia*, whose opinion of Alfonso's personal interest in the compilation is more in harmony with modern criticism (D. IV, 566-67, Castille, Alphonse X de, K). Of course Bayle did not know Alfonso's works directly; if he had, he surely would have been more generous in his judgment.

A noteworthy achievement of his article on Alfonso X was to rectify the false statements that had been made about the Castilian king. Besides rejecting the long and fanciful version of Alfonso's irreverence and proving Spizelius in error about his death, he also noted that Alfonso I of Aragon and Naples had been confused with Alfonso X of Castile and that the attributes and accomplishments of each had been assigned to the other. Among those guilty of such errors were Moréri, Matthias, J. J. Hofman, and Nicolas Lloyd. He similarly pointed out the gross errors committed by le père Pierre de Saint-Romould concerning Alfonso's testament and succession,[9] regretting that the passage by Saint-Romould had already been used as a source by l'Enfant and that it would probably serve as such for many other compilers (ibid.).

Turning to Bayle's knowledge of peninsular writers, both in Spanish and Latin, we can make several general classifications. First are the creative literary figures. Next are the historians. And next are the writers who were primarily religious and theological. This group will include a number of heretics, exiles from Spain or martyrs to their beliefs. Finally we might mention under the one heading of *érudits* a somewhat heterogeneous group including translators, doctors, philosophical writers, and compilers of facts. Some authors could appear under several of these headings. Mariana, for example, must be treated as a historian, as author of the *De Rege et Regis Institutione,* and as a Biblical commentator, for those are the aspects of his work that Bayle considers.

Pierre Bayle's great intellectual curiosity led him to read books of all kinds and he generally had something to say about everything he read. But his remarks are weakest in the field of imaginative literature. Most of the comments on purely literary Spanish works are found in the *Nouvelles de la République des Lettres,* where he reviewed new books and translations. One of the first notices of this type was that of the translation by Amelot de la Houssaie of Baltasar Gracián's *Oráculo Manual,* or *l'Homme de Cour,* as it was called in French (O.D. I, 97, N.R.L., July 1684). Bayle praised both the original author and the translator in this review. Of Gracián he wrote, "On sait que Gracian a été un génie d'une force et d'une élévation admirable," and he assured his readers that the translation would please all people of good taste. He relates a story about the Countess de Aranda, Luisa de Padilla, who was supposed to have regretted

---

[9] Among other things, Saint-Romould had claimed that Sancho was Alfonso's eldest son, that Alfonso left his kingdom to a younger son, that Sancho caused Alfonso's death in prison and killed his brother (D. IV, 567, Castille, Alphonse X de, L).

that Gracián's works were printed, "en sorte que le moindre bourgeois peut avoir pour un écu, des choses qui, à cause de leur excellence, ne sauraient être bien en de telles mains." He took this passage from the preface to *El discreto,* written by Gracián's friend, Juan de Lastanosa, and liked it so much that he later repeated it (D. XI, 328, Padilla, Louise de, A). Incidentally, Bayle preferred the French title of *l'Homme de Cour* because it was less ostentatious and hyperbolic and more indicative of the subject matter of the book. In the September, 1685, number of the *Nouvelles* is found a review of *La Semaine de Montalban, ou les mariages mal assortis,* by an anonymous translator. Bayle merely states that it is a very free translation, that everything not dealing with gallantry in the Spanish original has been deleted, and that much material has been added. In the same article he mentions another work of this nature, an anonymous *Histoire du temps, ou Journal Galant,* in which, he says, are found some horribly satiric passages about Spanish women. He adds that he does not know whether this is in reprisal against the calumnies of Spanish novelists or if the French authors are the aggressors (O.D. I, 381). The review of Baillet's *Jugement des Savants sur les principaux ouvrages des auteurs* offers comments on several Spanish writers. First is Juan de Mena, of whom Bayle writes that, had he lived in a more polished century, he could have restored to his native city of Cordoba the glory she had had under the Roman emperors. Next is Rodrigo Cota, "qui passe pour l'auteur de *la Celestina*" (no mention is made of Fernando de Rojas, now universally accepted as the author of most of the *Celestina).* Bayle discusses the Latin translation of the *Celestina* by Gaspar Barthius and the French one by Jacques de Lavardin du Plessis-Bourrot. Barthius, according to the author of the *Nouvelles,* was a great admirer of things Spanish and found no difficulty in calling the *Celestina* a "divine" book. Lavardin's translation, reprinted several times, does not give the same idea of the work. The comments on the great Portuguese poet, Luis de Camões, deal mainly with his life, the shipwreck and the saving of the *Lusiadas.* The author calls him the greatest poetic spirit of his age and regrets that his fame was not fully established until after his death. Góngora is referred to briefly as "un génie fort élevé," but it is Lope de Vega who is represented as the most diligent writer who ever existed. Even the Roman poet Lucius, who could write two hundred verses while standing on one foot, could not compare with the Spaniard (O.D. I, 757-58,

N.R.L., Feb. 1687). Of course, Bayle was merely repeating here the judgments of Baillet, but at least he found them interesting enough to pass on to his readers. Of these writers, the only one to whom he refers elsewhere was Lope, whose poem on the art of writing comedies he quoted in the *Continuation des pensées diverses*. Bayle's attitude toward the theatre was that its aim was to please: "On doit considérer la Comédie comme un repas donné au peuple; l'importance est donc que les viandes paraissent bonnes aux conviés, et non pas qu'elles aient été apprêtées selon les règles de l'art de Cuisine" (O.D. III, 202). Therefore Lope was justified in accommodating his genius even to women and ignorant people: "C'est par le même principe de s'accommoder plutôt au goût de ceux pour qui l'on écrit, qu'au goût des savants, que Lopes [sic] de Vega qui n'avait point trouvé son compte à faire des Comédies selon les règles, prit une autre route, et s'accommoda au génie des femmes et des ignorants" (ibid.).

A writer to whom Bayle devoted considerable space in the *Dictionnaire* was Juan de Espinosa. As we have previously stated, Bayle read the *Gynaecepaenos, o Diálogo en laude de las mugeres* in the Spanish edition printed at Milan in 1580, quoting extensively from the preface by Jerónimo Serrano. He devotes most of the article to a discussion of Espinosa's life, detailing his services to the Marqués de Alarcón and later to Pedro González de Mendoza and his position under the latter as Secretary of Affairs of State in Sicily. He takes up Espinosa's literary accomplishments in the notes. Although he finds that the *Diálogo* has too many examples and citations and suffers from a lack of selectivity, he expresses the desire to see the continuation of it, promised by the author, in which the famous women of the sixteenth century would be praised. He speaks favorably of a passage, which he quotes, in which Espinosa discusses literary critics. His words, according to Bayle, are filled with good sense and teach one to distinguish between censure which is of value and that which serves no purpose (D. XIII, 413, Spinosa, Jean de, B). Bayle also reports that Espinosa's collection of Spanish proverbs was not printed and had been lost. In connection with this last comment he lists various collections of proverbs, among which the Spanish ones are the *Refranes* of Hernán Núñez, the *Filosofía vulgar* of Juan de Mal-lara, the erudite disciple of Núñez, and the *Medicina española contenida en proverbios vulgares de nuestra lengua* of Jean Soropán de Rieros. His knowledge of these collections was gained from Morhof's *Polyhistor* (D. XIII, 415).

The *Dictionnaire* also has an article on Enrique de Villena, dealing with his life and reputation rather than with his works. Bayle relied almost entirely on Mariana in discussing this controversial figure. He says that Villena's works were very learned, but that they were written in a poor style. He relates how his library was examined and almost completely burned under the direction of Lope de Barrientos, confessor of Juan II of Castile, because of Villena's reputation as a necromancer. He strongly attacks Mayerne Turquet for supposing that only Villena's manuscripts on magic were burned, and says that if Turquet had taken the trouble to read Mariana more thoroughly, he would have written with more care (D. XIV, 412, Villena, C).

As can be seen, Bayle's knowledge of Spanish creative literature was varied, but undeniably limited. Much of what he knew was secondhand. We can be sure only that he read Gracián, the *Celestina*, and Pérez de Montalbán in translation, and Espinosa and, possibly, Lope de Vega in the original Spanish. One is struck by the complete absence (or, at most, only the most cursory mention) of the names of some of Spain's greatest writers, particularly those of the Golden Age. Cervantes, as we have said, is named only in a footnote. The dramatists, Tirso de Molina, Alarcón, Calderón, were apparently unknown to Bayle. Neither are Quevedo or Saavedra Fajardo considered by him. Several explanations of these omissions are possible. In the first place, many of Bayle's comments on more purely literary works are found in the *Nouvelles de la République des Lettres*, and his sources of information while he was editing that notable journal were limited. Almost all of the works reported were published in Holland. Not only Spanish books but even those published in France were difficult to obtain.[10] As for the *Dictionnaire*, we might point out that it was the author's avowed purpose not to repeat what could be found accurately recorded in Moréri and other dictionaries. Thus some of the omissions might be explained in this way. Nevertheless, the most probable answer should be sought in Bayle's own personality and his concept of literature. Pierre Bayle, possessing as he did many admirable qualities and abilities, was not a person of artistic discernment. He was interested in literature as a clear presentation of facts rather than as a matter

[10] Edmonde Lacoste, *Bayle nouvelliste et critique littéraire* (Bruxelles, 1929), pp. 66-69.

of esthetics, as scholarship rather than as creative art. He was indifferent, if not opposed, to poets and poetry, and saw little of value in novels. To him, one novel was as good as another. He was somewhat more interested in the drama, but here, too, the same general attitude is evident. Even though he enjoyed, to some extent, reading or seeing plays, this was not the type of literature he would be likely to seek out. Morever, in view of his insistence on accuracy of facts in whatever form they were presented (he objected to historical novels for their mingling of fact and fantasy), one can well imagine that the Spanish dramas of the Golden Age, based so often on historical incidents or using the names of historical persons, would have been harshly criticized had he turned his attention to them.

The situation is vastly different when we consider his awareness of Spanish historians. History was a field in which he was immensely interested and his knowledge of Spanish historical writings was considerable. His main source for the history of Spain was Mariana's *Historiae de Rebus Hispaniae*, but he knew, directly or indirectly, at least a dozen other Spanish historians. For the early history of Spain he relied almost entirely on Mariana, although he did know, probably through le père l'Enfant, of the work of Rodrigo Sánchez de Arévalo (D. IV, 565 ff, Castille, Alphonse X de, H and K) as well as a Latin chronicle of Aragon which he read in the *Hispania Illustrata* of Schottus (ibid., 564, F). Even the name of Diego de Valera was not unknown to him, although he admittedly cited him at third hand, at least.[11] It was in the history of Spain of the preceding two centuries that Bayle read most widely. For one thing, he reveals the contemporary interest in works on the New World and the Spanish conquests. In the *Nouvelles* of May, 1685, he reviewed a translation, *Histoire de la Conquête de la Floride par les Espagnols sous Ferdinand de Soto, écrite en Portugais par un Gentilhomme de la Ville d'Elvas et traduit* [sic] *en Français par M. D. C. (de la Guette de Citri)*. He notes that the history of the conquest of Florida by the Inca Garcilaso de la Vega had already been translated, but he feels that this work must be superior to the Inca's, both because the Portuguese gentleman took part in the principal events and deliberations of the enterprise and because he has avoided what Bayle calls "les exagérations

[11] Bayle mentions Valera in a quotation from the *Histoire Chronologique d'Espagne* of Mlle. XX (de la Roche), Rotterdam, 1694, which, in turn, was based on Mariana (D. XI, 323, Padilla, Marie de, C).

Espagnoles qui paraissent en très grand nombre dans Garcilasso" (O.D. I, 295). Bayle knew the history of Peru of Pedro Cieza de León in the Italian translation, edition of Venice, 1557. Although he gives no judgment of the work, it is evident that he found it worth-while, for he quoted extensively from it to prove his own point that the Indians of America were not corrupted by the Europeans (D. IX, 164 ff, Leon, Pierre Cieça de). Other works of peninsular travelers mentioned are the *Histoire de l'Ethiopie Orientale* of the Portuguese Dominican João dos Santos (O.D. I, 402, N.R.L., Oct. 1685) and the *Histoire de la Chine* of the Augustinian Juan González de Mendoza (D. X, 406, Mendozza).

The historians whom he knew best, other than Mariana, were those of Charles V and Philip II. He cites the works of Prudencio de Sandoval, Luis de Avila y Zúñiga, Antonio de Herrera, Alonso de Ulloa (who wrote in Italian), Juan Antonio de Vera y Figueroa, Conde de la Roca, as well as the *Vita di Carlo Quinto* of Lodovico Dolce, the *Historiae sui temporis* of Paolo Giovio, and the history of Philip's wars in Flanders by Cesare Campana (See D. V, 63ff, Charles-Quint; IV, 476 ff, Carranza; XI, 325 ff Padilla, Jean de). In a letter to Jacques Basnage dated November 17, 1674, Bayle told of having read La Mothe le Vayer's criticism of Sandoval's history of Charles V:

Que je prends plaisir à le voir dauber la partialité des historiens et que je suis aise de me voir délivré, par la lecture de ce livre, d'une erreur où j'ai été fort longtemps, de croire qu'il n'y avait que les historiens français qui mentissent en faveur de leur nation! Sandoval témoigne une partialité si énorme pour l'Espagne et contre la France, qu'il me contraint d'avouer que notre Gazette et son histoire ne s'en doivent guère l'une à l'autre .... (Emile Gigas, *Choix de la corresp. inéd. de P. Bayle*, Copenhague, 1890, p. 81; see also a letter to his older brother dated Nov. 23, 1674, O.D. I, 31).

His opinion of Sandoval never changed, unless it was to become even more unfavorable. In the *Pensées diverses* he attacked the Spaniard's credulity on two points—for attributing the piety of Queen Margarita, wife of Philip III, to the fact that she was born on Christmas Day and for reporting the various wonderful happenings that took place after the death of Charles V. He ironically laments that Sandoval should have forgotten the comet that appeared in the year the emperor died (although he slyly points out that the Conde de la Roca did report it) (O.D. III, 62). A few pages later he reproaches Spanish historians for their hyperbolic imaginations, which are si outrées, qu'au lieu de relever le mérite de ce grand prince, on peut dire qu'elles font tort à [sa] gloire .... C'est un Sandoval, historiographe de Philippe III et Evêque de Pampelone, qui dit de plus que le jour de la bataille [contre le duc de Saxe, 1547] le soleil fut vu de couleur de sang en France, en Allemagne et en Piémont; c'est un Don Louis d'Avila ... qui ... parle de ce prodige comme témoin oculaire ... . (O.D. III, 64).

In the *Nouvelles de la République des Lettres* of August, 1686, he returns to the attack, criticizing Sandoval and a certain Peñafiel Contreras for their daring in having respectively derived the genealogies of Philip III and the Duque de Lerma from Adam (O.D. I, 618). His attitude is recapitulated in the *Dictionnaire*:

Si le sujet [i.e. Charles] était grand, l'imagination et la rhétorique des Espagnols le furent aussi; et sûrement les historiens de ce prince auraient plus honoré sa mémoire, s'ils avaient donné plus de bornes à leurs louanges. Une page de M. de Thou est préférable à un volume de Sandoval, parce que M. de Thou, bon français, n'est point suspect de flatterie (D. V, 63, Charles-Quint).

Bayle accuses Sandoval and the Conde de la Roca of having falsified history in their accounts of the death of Charles V and the role played at his deathbed by Bartolomé de Carranza. In order to lessen the suspicion that the emperor was influenced by Carranza, later tried for harboring Lutheran convictions, the Spanish writers claimed that Charles had Carranza come in order to censure him on his erroneous opinions. Needless to say, Bayle does not favor this explanation (D, IV, 478, Carranza, C).

Another writer whom he attacked vigorously and frequently was Antonio de Guevara. Although Guevara held the post of chronicler to Charles V, he really was not a historian, but rather a moralist, putting his concept of society into literary forms that would be agreeable to his readers. Bayle was utterly incapable of comprehending such a purpose and treated Guevara only as a historian. Therefore his judgment of him is probably the harshest that he ever wrote of any author. To him the Bishop of Mondoñedo was "un empoisonneur public, et un séducteur, et, dans le tribunal de la république des lettres, il méritait le chatiment des profanes et des sacrilèges, car il violait ce qu'il y a de plus sacré dans l'art historique" (D. VII, 322, Guevara, B). Bayle praised Pedro de Rúa for his criticism of Guevara (ibid.; also D. XII, 644, Rua), and said that the latter's defense (Guevara claimed that, with the exception of holy Scripture, all history was so vague that one did not have to confirm or deny it) was, in his words, covering his nudity with fig leaves. He rails against Guevara's *pyrrhonisme historique*:

un auteur ne doit point se faire des règles particulières; c'est à lui à se conformer aux règles publiques: or, selon les lois publiques, en fait de lecture d'histoire, on reçoit pour bon ce qui se prouve par le témoignage des auteurs graves, et l'on rejette comme une fable tout ce qu'un moderne débite concernant l'antiquité, sans l'avoir lu dans de bons historiens. Ainsi, de quelque façon que Guévara considérât l'ancienne histoire, qu'il la crût vraie, qu'il la crût fausse, qu'il la crût douteuse, il devait citer ce qu'il y trouvait, et n'alleguer que cela, faute de quoi il mérite d'être traité comme un séducteur public (D. VII, 324, Guevara, D).

Besides reporting Rúa's censure of Guevara, Bayle quotes Andreas Schottus, Matamoros, Vossius, Gerardus Rupert, and Melchor Cano, all of whom offered objections to the *Marco Aurelio*. Nicolás Antonio in this case was too indulgent (ibid., 322 B). Style usually did not impress the author of the *Dictionnaire*, but even this he found objectionable in Guevara, calling it, because of its bad taste and false idea of eloquence, a "style ampoulé, figuré, plein d'antithèses." This was a minor point, however, compared to the extravagance with which Guevara dared to treat history (ibid., 321). He was celebrated for his eloquence, but according to Bayle he made himself ridiculous writing books.

Bayle was astounded at the eagerness of foreigners to translate Guevara's works. He admitted that many Frenchmen had been duped by the *Epístolas familiares* and that the *Reloj de príncipes o Marco Aurelio* had had a happy reception in France. Nevertheless, if the French were guilty of having paid so much attention to these works, the Spanish were even more culpable, for they esteemed them most. This last comment was not added to the article on Guevara until the third, and posthumous, edition of the *Dictionnaire*. In view of the many translations, French, Italian, and Latin, which Bayle listed[12] and which attested to the international popularity of Guevara, this judgment seems merely a weak attempt to assert national superiority.

Besides the long and unfavorable article on Guevara there are several other references to him in the *Dictionnaire*. In the article on Jean de Courres, the "Spanish imposter" is named as the poisoned source from which the author of the *Oeuvres morales et diversifiées* drew his falsifications (D. IV, 605, Courres, A). Thomas Elyot was probably encouraged in his fraudulent history of the Emperor Alexander by the success that Guevara's *Marco Aurelio* enjoyed (D. VI, 157, Encolpius, A). Guevara's errors concerning the courtesan Laïs are pointed out in the article of that name, and the mistakes later committed by Brantôme and

---

[12] These are listed in Appendix II.

du Verdier Vau-Privas are explained by their having accepted Guevara as a trustworthy source (D. IX, 25, Laïs, V).

In view of Bayle's unfavorable attitude toward Guevara, and remembering especially that he subscribed to Montaigne's opinion about the *Epístolas familiares* ("Ceux qui les ont appelées dorées faisaient jugement bien autre que celui que j'en fais") in his article on the Spanish writer (D. VII, 326, Guévara, H), it is surprising to find that he used these same *Epístolas* as a source for his article on Juan de Padilla. He quoted, from the French translation of Guterry, letters of Guevara to María de Padilla and don Antonio de Zúñiga, not only accepting them at face value but even preferring Guevara as a source over Brantôme (D. XI, 325 ff, Padilla, Jean de). This is the only occasion on which he spoke well of Guevara. Elsewhere he considered him no better than a liar, dangerous not only because of his own falsehoods but also because of the example he set for other writers. It was Bayle's weakness that he could not see in Guevara the agreeable and cultured moralistic humanism which gave his works such wide appeal. He took Guevara's historical camouflage too seriously.

If the French savant's views on many Spanish historians, notably Sandoval, the Conde de la Roca, and Guevara, were unfavorable, this was more than compensated for by the praise which he gave to Juan de Mariana as a historian. Bayle was a difficult man to satisfy, and the fact that Mariana was generally accepted by him speaks much for the Jesuit's ability. He devoted a long article to Mariana in the *Dictionnaire* and there are references to the historian in his correspondence. He called him one of the ablest men of his century, "grand theologien, grand humaniste, profond dans la connaissance de l'histoire ecclésiastique et de l'histoire profane, bon grec, et docte dans la langue sainte (D. X, 257, Mariana). Elsewhere in the *Dictionnaire,* which abounds in references to Mariana, he praised him as a "sage historien" (D. IV, 565, Castille, Alphonse X de) and as "un des meilleurs historiens espagnols" (D. XIV, 490, Urraca, C). He preferred him as a source over Sánchez de Arévalo and le père l'Enfant for material on Alfonso X[13] and gave him credence over Mayerne Turquet on Enrique de Villena. He based his article on the mis-

---

[13] The article on Alfonso X is saturated with references to and direct quotations from Mariana: "Il me semble que mon lecteur ne doit pas être fâché de trouver ici les paroles dont Mariana s'est servi," "Voyons encore les expressions de Mariana," "Mariana dit en general que ... ," etc. etc.

tress of Pedro *el cruel* almost entirely on Mariana, saying, "Je ne renvoie point mon lecteur à *l'Histoire des Favorites,* imprimée l'an 1697; car ce qu'on y dit de notre Padilla est sophistiqué de mille contes romanesques. Ce n'est point dans de tels ouvrages qu'il faut chercher la verité, mais dans des auteurs comme Mariana" (D. XI, 322, Padilla, Marie de, C). In a letter dated February 13, 1696, to M. Rou, who was preparing a translation of Mariana's history, Bayle gently cautions his correspondent to be careful in criticizing the Spanish historian. Mariana, he says, is considered by the Jesuits and by the Spanish in general as one of their greatest men. Therefore Rou should not criticize him unless he is on sure ground, and he should foresee the resources that Mariana's defenders will have (O.D. IV, 721).

Reliance on Mariana for Spanish material increased with each new edition of the *Dictionnaire*. In the first edition (1696) Bayle used him as his main source for Alfonso X of Castile and Alfonso I of Naples and had already written the article on the historian himself. In the second edition (1701) he added articles on several more Spanish figures, María de Padilla, Urraca, and Enrique de Villena, all of which were based primarily on Mariana. Also in the second edition the article on Mariana was increased considerably by the addition of a final paragraph and five more notes (notes F, K, M, O, and P). The article on Alfonso Espina, based largely on Mariana, did not appear until the third edition (1720).

In his criticism of Mariana's history Bayle relied considerably on the favorable comments that le père Rapin had published in his *Réflexions sur l'Histoire*. Rapin had especially praised Mariana for "une sagesse qui ne lui permet jamais de s'abandonner aux beaux endroits, ni de se négliger en ceux qui ne le sont pas: cette égalité si judicieuse, qui est toujours la même dans l'inégalité des matières que touche cet auteur ... ." (quoted by Bayle, D. X, 260, Mariana, C). Bayle quotes three other long passages from Rapin, all favorable to the author of the *Historiae de Rebus Hispaniae*. For his own part, he lauds Mariana's refusal to continue his history up to his own time. The *Historiae* ended at the death of Ferdinand of Aragon, with only a summary in the appendix of events from then until the time the book was written. Mariana did not wish to continue his history further for the obvious reason that it would be necessary to write about people still living and it would be difficult to maintain his objectivity and impartiality. Bayle agreed: "C'est le parti le plus sûr et le plus honnête, et celui que les gens sages ont toujours le plus approuvé" (D. X, 260, Mariana, C). He mentioned that the *Historiae* had been criticized by Pedro Mantuano and that the criticism was answered by Tomás Tamayo de Vargas. He repeated, using Nicolás Antonio as his source, Tamayo de Vargas' story of how Mariana wished to see neither the work of his detractor nor that of his apologist (ibid.). Bayle knew the *Advertencias* of Mantuano, but regretted that he had not seen the defense by Tamayo de Vargas (D. X, 260, Mariana, B; O.D. IV, 723, letter to M. Rou dated Feb. 21, 1696). The fact that Mariana himself translated his history into Spanish, revising and changing from the original, was also reported, Antonio again being the source (D. X, 260, Mariana, C). Finally he referred his readers to the *Abrégé Chronologique de l'Histoire d'Espagne*, based principally on Mariana, which was published in Holland in 1694 and was attributed to a Mlle. de la Roche, and also called attention to the forthcoming French translation of Mariana's history by M. Rou, announced in November of 1693.[14]

Bayle's admiration for Mariana the historian was clear and unequivocal. This is evident in the praise he gave him in the article bearing his name, in the considerable number of articles based on his work, and in the fact that he accepted his statements even over those of French historians and on at least two occasions developed moral themes from Mariana's history, willingly admitting where he found them, as in the statement on the evil effects of lust for power (D. IV, 562, Castille, Alphonse X de) and in his consideration on the changes of Fortune (D. XI, 281, Naples, Alphonse I de, A). But he also considered another aspect of the Spanish Jesuit, that is, as the author of the controversial *De Rege et Regis Institutione*. Here Bayle's attitude is not so clear. Although the few opinions that he had on politics are said to have been monarchical,[15] his attitude toward the *De Rege* lends itself to varying interpretations. The pivotal point of Mariana's book, the point that caused it to be burned in Paris, was concerned with the question of whether the people have the right to depose and even to assassinate a tyrant. Mariana's fundamental theory was that the authority of the people is superior to that of kings, and therefore even a private individual has the right to kill a wicked sovereign. Bayle calls this doctrine pernicious and se-

[14] As far as I know, Rou's translation never appeared.
[15] Horatio E. Smith, *The Literary Criticism of Pierre Bayle* (Albany, 1912), p. 132.

ditious. Pointing out that Mariana approved the action of Jacques
Clément, the assassin of Henry III, he warns:

Cette observation découvre admirablement tout le venin de la doctrine de ce
jésuite; car il est certain qu'il ne débute par l'exemple de Henri III que pour
descendre de la thèse à l'hypothèse et pour montrer aux peuples un cas insigne
de tyrannie, afin que toutes les fois qu'ils se trouveront en semblable état, ils
se croient dans les circonstances où il est permis de faire jouer le couteau contre
leurs monarques (D. X, 264, Mariana, G).

He also attacks with vigor the fact that Mariana distinguished
between two ways of poisoning a tyrant. The Spaniard had written that it is permissible to put poison on his clothes, saddle, etc.,
but not in his food or drink (the purpose was to guard against
any possibility of suicide, which would endanger the victim's
soul). Bayle calls these distinctions ridiculous, and is surprised
that a writer of such good sense and such logic could have fallen
into so puerile an argument (ibid., 266). It should be noted,
however, that by the time he gets to this criticism he has very
cleverly and very thoroughly repeated for his readers all of
the arguments that Mariana set forth in his discussion. As to the
question of the sovereignty of the people versus the divine right
of kings, he says he will not enter the argument. Nevertheless he
refers the reader to remark "S" under "Loyola" (ibid.), where
he attacks the Jesuits for using both doctrines, i.e., kings receive
the right to stamp out heresy from God, and if the king is remiss
in this, the people are justified in overthrowing him (D. IX, 327
ff, Loyola, S).

One might conclude from this that Bayle was definitely antiMariana, but his next note makes one wonder. Here he considers
various attacks and defenses of the *De Rege*. Particularly he
criticizes a Lutheran writer, Seckendorf, who claimed that Mariana's doctrine was a defense of assassination of heretical kings,
either because of the zeal of the individual or on orders from the
Pope. Bayle points out that Mariana says nothing about heretical
rulers or permission or commands from Rome: "Ses maximes
regardent toutes les nations et tous les tyrans: il n'exclut point
de ses règles les protestants qui se trouveraient sous un règne
tyrannique; il n'en exclut point les Mahometans ni les paiens;
il traite cette question tout comme aurait fait Aristote." (D. X,
271, Mariana, K). As for the example of Jacques Clément,
Bayle states that this was merely in Mariana's preamble and that
it is not his precise doctrine (ibid.). Furthermore, the argument
that Ravaillac had read Mariana's book before he made an at-

tempt on the life of Henry IV is shown to be unsupportable (ibid.). Finally, he points out that there are other works more pernicious than that of Mariana (ibid., 264, Mariana, G). This discussion of Mariana seems typical of Bayle's method in handling controversial matters. The article itself and even some of the notes would lead one to think that his attitude toward the *De Rege et Regis Institutione* was decidedly one of condemnation. Yet, when we read carefully everything that he has to say about the author and the work, we find attenuations, justifications, and even praise, exactly opposite of what he had previously written. Hence, if the reader could not conclude what Bayle's precise attitude was, the article nevertheless would make him ponder the problem. It seems to this writer that Bayle's real admiration for Mariana's logic is veiled under picayune criticisms of a few minor points.

There is a brief discussion of other works by Mariana, his treatise on the monetary system of Spain, the *Del Gobierno de la Compañia de Jesús,* and his commentaries on the Bible. Bayle repeats le père Simon's judgment that Mariana was one of the ablest scholiasts of the Bible (D. X, 274, Mariana, N).

Pierre Bayle's knowledge of theologians, preachers, and religious controversialists of Spanish origin was broad. Religious controversy was among the subjects he was most interested in and he was well versed in the writings of Spain's theologians. But here, too, his treatment is uneven. One of the best known, Melchor Cano, is mentioned only casually, although favorably, for his critical opinion on the legendary character of some saints' lives (D. XI, 564, Pérez, Joseph, A)[16] or in connection with a story about the Jesuits and Philip II (D. X, 260, Mariana, C), whereas some secondary figures are given more prominent notice. One of the earliest mentions of a Spanish religious writer is in a letter to his brother Jacob, dated November 2, 1670, in which he speaks of having read three treatises of Juan de España, the Jewish convert and author of polemical works in favor of Christianity. He termed his work "fort bon et d'un critique très profitable."[17] In the *Dictionnaire* there are articles, usually short, on José Pérez, professor of theology at Salamanca, Alfonso Espina, Jewish convert and Franciscan, Juan Andrés, Moham-

---

[16] Bayle also refers to Luis Vives' criticism of the zeal which falsifies saints' lives, quoting from his *De Disciplinis* (D. IX, 31, Lambert, B).

[17] J. L. Gerig and G. L. van Roosbroeck, "Unpublished letters of Pierre Bayle," *Romanic Review,* XXIII (July-Sept. 1932), 220.

medan convert, Juan de Cartagena, Jesuit and later Franciscan, and González Ponce de León, panegyrist of the popes, as was Cartagena. For the most part, Bayle limits himself to a brief biographical notice of each, with a list of their works. Alfonso Espina's *Fortalitium Fidei* is dismissed with the unfavorable criticism of du Pin (D. XIII, 410, Spina, Alphonse, A), but the *Confusion de la secte de Mahumed* by Juan Andrés is found to be quite good. Bayle notes that all who write against the Mohammedans refer to it, says that it has been translated into various languages, and reveals that he himself used the French version which Guy le Fèvre de la Boderie made of the Italian translation (D. II, 86, André, Jean, A and B). The most interesting comment about Ponce de León is that he did not write bad Latin for a Spaniard. He explains in a note: "Je ne veux pas dire qu'il n'y ait des Espagnols qui ont très bien entendu la langue latine, et qui s'en sont servis purement et éloquemment. Ma pensée est que pour l'ordinaire les écrivains de cette nation se négligent trop là-dessus" (D. IX, 168, Léon, Gonzales Ponce de, A). There is also an article on the Portuguese savant, Diego de Payva de Andrade, a theologian, preacher, and defender of the Council of Trent. For the most part it deals with the controversy in print between Andrade and his adversary, Martin Chemnitz (D. II, 79 ff, Andrada).

The writer in this category who received the greatest attention from the author of the *Dictionnaire* was Luis de León. The fact that Fray Luis spent some years in the jails of the Inquisition did not lessen Bayle's interest in him. Bayle reviews his life, comments on his command of Greek and Hebrew, and credits him with great "dexterity" in his explanations of the lessons of the Bible. He attributes León's imprisonment to his explanation of a particular verse of the Song of Songs, the lines "Je suis tombée entre les mains de ceux qui veillent pour la garde de la ville, et ils m'ont dépouillée; ceux qui en défendent les murailles m'ont blessée." Of course, the translation and comments on the Song of Songs did figure in the charges against Fray Luis, but that was only one of the accusations. Bayle saw in the commentary a vigorous attack against ecclesiastical authority, basing his opinion on what was said in the *Avis sincères aux Catholiques des Provinces-Unies*. He remarked that persecution sharpens the spirit and gives admirable openings to the mystic sense (D. IX, 164, Léon, C).

Among the writers whom Bayle treated are a number of heretics—Bartolomé Carranza, Francisco de Enzinas, or Dryander, and his brother Jaime, Constantino Ponce de la Fuente, Miguel de Montserrate, and Juan de Valdés. Carranza, archbishop of Toledo and confessor of Charles V, was arrested by the Inquisition for harboring heretical views. The fact that he had been present at the death of the emperor led to no little speculation as to the religious convictions of the latter. Bayle reported both sides of the question in detail, but took Spanish historians to task for attempting to deny or mitigate the effects of the relationship between Carranza and Charles V (D. IV, 476 ff, Carranza). As for the brothers Dryander, Bayle was mainly concerned with the martyrdom of Jaime, although he tells in a note that Francisco produced a Spanish translation of the New Testament which was dedicated to Charles V, "ce qui fit grand bruit dans les Pays-Bas" (D. VI, 17, Dryander). The article on Constantino Ponce deals with his life, works, and death. Bayle lists his *Confesión del pecador* and the *Summa de doctrina christiana*, as well as his sermons and commentaries on the Bible, taking most of his information from Nicolás Antonio. He also says that he read the life of Ponce, written in Latin by Reinaldo González de Montes, the panegyrist of Doctor Constantino (D. XII, 244, Ponce). It has already been noted that the Rotterdam sceptic read the *Aviso sobre los abusos de la Iglesia Romana* in Spanish and that he quoted from Montserrate passages not at all flattering to Spanish clerics.

Under Juan de Valdés are given both the works of the religious reformer and those of his brother Alfonso. Bayle merely followed his sources, mainly the *Bibliothèque française* of du Verdier Vau-Privas, and made no distinction between the author of *Las ciento diez consideraciones divinas* and the author of the *Diálogo de Mercurio y Carón* and the *Diálogo de Lactancio y un arcediano*, although he did note that the *Diálogos* are two separate works—not one, as had been said (D. XIV, 309, Valdès, Jean, E). Juan de Valdés is identified as one of the first founders of Lutheranism in the Kingdom of Naples. He received honors from Charles V, probably acquired his opinions against the Roman Church during a trip to Germany, and had great influence on some people of the upper class, including members of the clergy, who attended his secret assemblies. But "l'inquisition s'en aperçut, et par les remèdes violents qu'elle employa selon sa coutume, elle dissipa ces commencements de réformation" (ibid., 306). As for Valdés' doctrines, Bayle realized that they did not conform strictly either to Catholicism or to Protestantism. He adds that this author's works were placed on the *Index*, and lists the translations in French, Italian, and English of which he has found notice.

Finally we come to those Spanish writers considered by Bayle whom we have grouped together as *érudits*. Bayle was familiar with, or at least aware of, the works of many learned Spaniards of the sixteenth and seventeenth centuries, most of whom wrote in Latin. Some have already been mentioned: Hernán Núñez and Juan de Mal-lara for their collections of proverbs, José Pérez, the historian of the Benedictines, Pedro de Rúa, the critic of Guevara, and others. There remain the authors of various treatises, classical scholars or translators, philosophers, and the great bibliographer, Nicolás Antonio. In the *Réponse aux Questions d'un Provincial*, Bayle, in a supposed reply to his questioner, gives considerable information on the life of Francisco Ramos del Manzano (Ramón Sforcia Casini), professor of law at Salamanca and author of the *Respuesta de España al manifiesto de Francia*. He regrets not having Antonio at hand for his information, for the latter had been Manzano's student and esteemed him highly. He notes that most of Manzano's works were in manuscript and refers his reader to the commentary of José Fernández de Retes, also professor of law at Salamanca, for the praise that had been given to Manzano (O.D. III, 555). Also mentioned in the *Réponse* is Martín Antonio del Río, born in Antwerp of Basque parents. Bayle again refers the reader to another source, this time Alegambe's *Bibliotheca scriptorum Societatis Jesu*, for the catalogue of del Río's works, mentioning only two Latin books that were published posthumously under pseudonyms (O.D. III, 524). It should be noted that del Río's best known work, the *Disquisitionum Magicarum*, was used by Bayle as a source for his article on "Zahuris" in the *Dictionnaire* (D. XV, 16-17, Zahuris). Of Tomás Sánchez, the erudite Jesuit author of *De Sacramento matrimonii*, he says, "Son érudition n'est pas douteuse." Although Sánchez was attacked for including in his treatise passages of questionable taste, many had written in defense of his work. Bayle was particularly impressed by Nicolás Antonio's praise for his exactitude in quoting his sources, a talent which the author of the *Dictionnaire* considered much rarer than is generally thought (D. XIII, 76 ff, Sanchez, Thomas). The article on Baltasar Alamos de Barrientos, translator of Tacitus, is mainly biographical, dealing with his disgrace after the fall of Antonio Pérez, his imprisonment for eleven years, and his rehabilitation (D. I, 355), Alamos). Again Bayle relies on Nicolás Antonio for his information and offers no judgment of his own as to Barrientos' literary merits. He probably did not know his works directly. On the other hand, he had read the *Hypomnemata in C. Valerium Martialem* of Lorenzo Ramírez de Prado, with whose note to a passage by the Latin epigramist he disagreed (O.D. III, 365, Continuation des Pensées diverses, note Y).

Two Spanish doctors and philosophical writers who were known to Bayle were Gómez Pereira and Juan Huarte de San Juan. The former, author of the notable *Antoniana Margarita*, was fond of paradox, so much so that Bayle says, "la liberté de philosopher était pour lui un grand charme; il s'en servit amplement, jusqu'à l'abus." He discusses several of Pereira's main theses, especially the idea he set forth that animals are only machines without feeling. He rejects categorically the claim that Descartes took this paradox from Pereira, insisting that the French writer had never heard of the Spaniard. He affects the utmost astonishment that any writer as daring in his ideas as Pereira could have come forth in Spain, and states that he formed no school and that his work was practically unknown in his—that is, Bayle's —time (O.D. I, 7, N.R.L., March 1684; D. XI, 546, Péréira).

Bayle knew the *Examen de ingenios para las ciencias* of Juan Huarte both in an Italian version and in the French translation of Gabriel Chappuis, for he specifically mentions having used both. He was also acquainted with the criticism of the work by Jourdain Guibelet, the *Examen de l'Examen des Esprits*. He himself praises Huarte for his independence of thought, his profound meditation, and his discernment, but he advises caution in accepting either the maxims of the *Examen* or the authorities whom the author claimed he was using. He seems to feel that Huarte's general ideas are valid but that it would be difficult to put them into practice. He notes, incidentally, that although Huarte passed for a Spaniard, he was really born at St. Jean Pied-de-Port, in French Navarre (D. VIII, 292 ff, Huarte, Jean).

The Spaniard to whom Bayle was most indebted for material on peninsular writers was the learned bibliographer don Nicolás Antonio. Although his acquaintance with the work of Antonio came rather late, the many references to the *Bibliotheca Hispana Nova* and, to a lesser extent, to the *Vetus* show that he made good use of them once he had obtained the two parts of this monumental work. From what Bayle himself wrote it is possible to date fairly precisely the period in which he used the *Bibliotheca* of Antonio. At the time he was composing the article on Antonio for the first edition of the *Dictionnaire,* which came out in 1696, Bayle had seen neither of the parts of the *Bibliotheca.* He knew that the second part, the *Nova,* had been completed but he did not know whether the author had finished the *Vetus* (D. II, 154, Antonio). Consequently his article on Antonio was very short and dealt mainly with his early life and his work on false chronicles. Between the time when he wrote the article on Antonio and the time when the first edition of the *Dicionnaire* was published he evidently borrowed a copy of the *Nova,* for several of the articles in the first edition—those on Bartolomé Carranza, Juan de Cartagena, Pedro Cieza de León, Francisco Sánchez, and Pedro de Rúa—have references to Nicolás Antonio. For the second edition Bayle expanded the article on Antonio, doubling the size and adding four long notes. He included details about Antonio's life, notably his work at the royal monastery of the Escorial, and about the publication of the *Bibliotheca,* material which he obtained from the *Journal des Savants* of June 10, 1697 (D. II, 155). That he had borrowed a copy of the *Nova* is made clear by what he wrote in the *Réponse aux Questions d'un Provincial,* the *avertissement* of which is dated September 28, 1703. Discussing Francisco Ramos del Manzano he wrote:

Si j'avais la Bibliothèque des Ecrivains Espagnols du 16 et du 17 siècle, je pense que je pourrais vous fournir beaucoup de choses; car Don Nicolas Antonio, l'auteur de cet excellent ouvrage, estimait beaucoup le jurisconsulte dont il s'agit. Il avait été son disciple et il en parle avec éloge dans son traité *de Exilio.* Malheureusement, je n'ai plus cette partie de sa Bibliothèque; je l'ai eue d'emprunt trois ou quatre ans; après quoi je l'ai rendue comme de raison à celui qui avait eu la bonté de me la prêter (O.D. III, 555).

Obviously he borrowed it while working on the *Dictionnaire.* As for the *Vetus,* Bayle had not yet seen it when he was preparing the additions to the second edition, although he did have some information about it, at least about the entries on the pseudo-chronicles of Dexter, Luitprandus, and Maximus, which he found in the *Apologia pro Veritate* of the Spanish Jesuit Antonio Jaramillo. But of the two volumes of the *Vetus* itself he wrote, "Je ne les ai point encore vus, et je doute qu'il y en ait aucun exemplaire dans les Provinces-Unies." Later, when he had obtained access to the *Vetus,* he added an explanatory note that he had written this on February 8, 1699 (D. II, 157).

Bayle's admiration for Nicolás Antonio was great and sincere. There is hardly an article on a Spanish writer for which he did not turn to the *Bibliotheca Hispana* for some facts. Specifically, there are at least eighteen articles in the *Dictionnaire*, from Abrabanel to Villareal, in which Nicolás Antonio appears as a source. It is to be expected that with so many references to Antonio, Bayle would find some faults in his work. Thus he disagrees with him as to the year of Mariana's death (D. X, 259, Mariana, A), censures him for saying nothing about the execution of Manuel Fernández de Villareal, who was burned as a Judaiser in Lisbon (D. XIV, 395, Villareal, A), remarks that he erred on the *Sermones* of Constantino Ponce (D. XII, 245, Ponce, B), and claims that he was too lenient in his judgment of Antonio de Guevara (D. VII, 323, Guevara, B). These are but minute criticisms, however. Most often he accepts Antonio's statements without question. Even before he knew the work directly, he praised the concept of the *Bibliotheca Hispana* and conceded that Spain in this respect had surpassed France in the person of Nicolás Antonio (O.D. I, 499-500, N.R.L., Feb. 1686). In his article on the Spanish savant in the enlarged version of the second edition he recommends the favorable review of the *Bibliotheca* by Baillet, and terms the review of it that appeared in the *Journal des Savants* of July 6, 1676, "un chétif article de cet excellent ouvrage." He says that Antonio has done his nation great honor with his work, and that no one has succeeded better than he in that sort of compilation. He commends Baillet for his praise, even of the various tables of contents that Antonio included, and comments on the good taste shown by Antonio in the preface to those tables (D. II, 154-55).

It was only natural that Bayle would be favorably impressed by Antonio's work, for in a sense they were kindred spirits; both were interested in facts and were indefatigable researchers. Moreover, Antonio's efforts to shed light on the false chronicles of Spain made him an agreeable figure in the eyes of Bayle, even though he wondered if Antonio had meant to touch on certain pious fables of his country (D. II, 154). He noted that the Jesuits had already complained about the *Vetus* (indirectly attacking Cardinal de Aguirre, who paid the expense of printing it) and feared there would be more attacks. Recalling that the Marqués de Agropoli (Gaspar Ibáñez de Segovia, Marqués de Mondejar) was denounced to the Inquisition for his attacks on the fabulous character of some histories, he concluded, "Je ne puis comprendre que les moines de ce pays-là soient capables de laisser en repos la mémoire de notre Nicolas Antonio" (D. II, 157, Antonio, D).

Bayle did not let any opportunity pass for an attack on the Spanish clergy.

There can be no doubt that Pierre Bayle had more than a superficial concern with things Spanish. He was aware of a number of currents in Spanish thought and gave his readers, particularly in the *Dictionnaire,* considerable information on the literature of the Iberian Peninsula. At the same time he furthered an unfavorable picture of the Spanish people. Although there is but scant evidence that he had any personal contact with them, his comments on Spanish character, habits, and outlook were uniformly disparaging. Fortunately his generalities about them were not too frequent. Bayle's opinions about the rulers of that nation were equally negative, and his dislike for the Spanish clergy led him to accept as true some stories of doubtful authenticity. But contrasted to what we must recognize as a personal aversion to Spain, we have his undeniable interest in her writers. While it can be pointed out that there is considerable unevenness in his treatment of Spanish letters, this can be explained at least partially by the fact that he set out to correct the errors in Moréri's *Grand Dictionnaire historique* and that he did not repeat information correctly presented there.

Bayle's comments on literary figures helped to make his audience aware of the existence of certain Iberian writers. The notices, both in the *Nouvelles de la République des Lettres* and in the *Dictionnaire,* of translations of Spanish and Portuguese works reflect the popularity that the writers of those nations enjoyed in the rest of Europe. His articles on religious and erudite writers of the peninsula offer ample proof of the wide scope of his knowledge about Hispanic letters. Of earlier historical personages treated in the *Dictionnaire,* the most important among the Spaniards was Alfonso X of Castile. The article on that monarch is noteworthy for its adherence to the generally accepted facts about his life and for the correction of inaccuracies that had been published about him. Bayle's treatment of Spanish historians was harsh, but not unjustifiably so. The truth is that the chroniclers of the House of Austria were often panegyrists rather than impartial recorders, and it cannot be denied that Sandoval and the Conde de la Roca were most credulous in reporting marvellous signs and portents. (In all truth, Bayle was just as naïve in accepting unsubstantiated tales about Spanish monks.) Although he was overly harsh in his treatment of Antonio de Guevara, Bayle was not the first nor the last to object to that writer's style and handling of history. Finally, his recognition of the merits of two great Spanish savants is evidence of his good critical judgment. There were no other writers on whom he could more safely rely for Spain's history and bibliographical notices than Juan de Mariana and Nicolás Antonio.

APPENDIX I

SPANISH AND PORTUGUESE WRITERS REFERRED TO IN THE WORKS OF BAYLE

Names are listed alphabetically according to their Spanish spelling. The words in parentheses are the titles of articles in which the reference may be found.

Alamos de Barrientos, Baltasar: Article D. I, 355.
Alarcón, Benito de: D. II, 79 (Andrada).
Alcázar, Luis de: Article D. I, 371.
Alfonso X: Article D. IV, 56 (Castille, Alphonse X roi de); O.D. I, 548 (N.R.L., May, 1686).
Andrade, Diego de Payva de: see Payva de Andrade.
Andrés, Juan: Article D. II, 86.
Antonio, Nicolás: Article D. II, 154; D. I. 83 (Abrabanel), 355 (Alamos), 372 (Alcasar); II, 439 (Arriaga); IV, 476 (Carranza), 482 (Cartagena, Jean), 566 (Castille, Alphonse X de, K): VI, 627 (Furius, Frideric, A); VII, 167 (Govéa), 321 ff (Guevara); IX, 164 (Léon, Pierre Cieça de); X. 2 (Macédo, François), 159 (Maldonat, Jean[2], A), 258 ff (Mariana), 486 (Monardes, A); XI, 546 (Pereira, Gomezius, B); XII, 244 (Ponce, Constantin), 644 (Rua, Pierre); XIII, 76 (Sanchez, François), 78 (Sanchez, Thomas, A), 414 (Spinosa, Jean de, B); XIV, 310 (Valdès, Jacques), 308 (Valdès, Jean de, E), 395 (Villareal, A); O.D. I, 499 (N.R.L., Feb. 1686); III, 555 (Réponse).
Arriaga, Rodrigo de: Article D. II, 437.
Avila y Zúñiga, Luis: O.D. III, 64 (Pensées diverses).
Camoes, Luis de: O.D. I, 758 (N.R.L., Feb. 1687).
Cano, Melchor: D. X, 260 (Mariana, C); XI, 564 (Perez, Joseph A).
Carranza de Miranda, Bartolomé: Article D. IV, 476.
Cartagena, Fr. Juan de: Article D. IV, 482.
Castro, Fr. Alonso de: D. V, 361 (Damascène, Jean, A).
Celestina: see Cota, Rodrigo.
Cervantes, Miguel de: D. II, 521 (Audiguier, A).
Cieza de León, Pedro: Article D. IX, 164.
Cota, Rodrigo, reputed author of the Celestina: O.D. I, 757 (N.R.L., Feb. 1687).
Dryander, Francisco: see Enzinas, Francisco de.
Enzinas, Francisco de: D, VI, 17 (Dryander, Jean, B).
España, Juan de: J. L. Gerig and G. L. van Roosbroeck, "Unpublished letters of Pierre Bayle," in Romanic Review, XXIII (July-Sept. 1932), 220 (letter to brother Jacob, Nov. 2, 1670).
Espina, Fr. Alonso de: Article D. XIII, 410 (Spina); D. IV, 565 (Castille, Alphonse de, G).
Espinosa, Juan de: Article D. XIII, 412 (Spinosa).
Fernández de Retes, José: O.D. II, 555 (Réponse).
Fernández de Villareal, Manuel: Article D. XIV, 395 (Villareal).

Furió Ceriol, Fadrique: Article D. VI, 627.
Galesinus, Petrus: Article D. VII, 4 (Gales, Pierre).
García, Dr. Carlos: O.D. III, 521 (Réponse).
García Matamoros, Alfonso: D. VII, 322 (Guevara, A).
Góngora y Argote, Luis de: O.D. I, 759 (N.R.L., Feb. 1687).
González de Mendoza, Juan: Article D. X, 406 (Mendoza).
González de Montes, Reinaldo: D. XII, 244 (Ponce, Constantin).
Gracián, Baltasar: D. XI, 328 (Padilla, Louise de, A); O.D. I, 97 (N.R.L., July 1684).
Guevara, Antonio de: Article D. VII, 321; D. IV, 605 (Courres, Jean des, A); VI, 157 (Encolpius, A); IX, 25 (Laïs, V); XI, 325 ff (Padilla, Jean de); XII, 644 (Rua, Pierre).
Gutiérrez, Juan Lázaro: D. XV, 16 (Zahuris).
Herrera, Antonio de: D. V, 76 (Charles-Quint, S).
Huarte de San Juan, Juan: Article D. VIII, 292.
Ibáñez de Segovia, Marqués de Mondejar: D. II, 157 (Antonio, D); "Lettres inédites de Pierre Bayle," *Revue d'Histoire Littéraire de la France*, XX, 432 (letter to l'abbé Dubos).
Jaramillo, Antonio Matías: D. II, 157 (Antonio, D).
Jiménez Guillén, Francisco: O.D. I, 566 (N.R.L., May 1686).
Lastanosa, Juan de: D. XI, 328 (Padilla, Louise de, A).
León, Gonzalvo Ponce de: *see* Ponce de León.
León, Fr. Luis de: Article D. IX, 162.
León, Pedro Cieza de: *see* Cieza de León.
Luna Vega, Juan de: O.D. I, 566 (N.R.L., May 1686).
Macedo, Antonio: Article D. X, 4.
Macedo, Francisco: Article D. X, 1.
Maldonado, Juan, Jesuit author: Article D. X, 158.
Maldonado, Juan, priest at Burgos: Article D. X, 157.
Mal-lara, Juan de: D. XIII, 415 (Spinosa, Jean de, B).
Mantuano, Pedro: D. X, 262 (Mariana, D); O.D. IV, 723 (letter to M. Rou, Feb. 21, 1696).
Mariana, Juan de: Article D. X, 257; D. II, 27 ff (Naples, Alphonse 1er de); IV, 562 ff (Castille, Alphonse X de); V, 302 (Coronel, Alphonse); XI, 320 ff (Padilla, Marie de); XIII, 410 (Spina, Alphonse, A); XIV, 412 (Villéna, C), 486 ff (Urraca); O.D. IV, 721 (letter to M. Rou, Feb. 13, 1696), 723 (letter to M. Rou, Feb. 21, 1696); Emile Gigas, *Choix de la Correspondance inédite de Pierre Bayle* (Copenhague, 1890), 112.
Mena, Juan de: O.D. I, 757 (N.R.L., Feb. 1687).
Mendoza, Juan González de: *see* González de Mendoza.
Molina, Luis de: O.D. I, 668 (N.R.L., Oct. 1686); III, 409 (Continuation des Pensées diverses).
Monardes, Nicolás: Article D. X, 485.
Montalbán, Juan Pérez de: *see* Pérez de Montalbán.
Montemayor, Jorge de: D. II, 39 (Antoine, Marc, A).
Montserrate, Miguel de: Article D. X, 490.
Núñez, Hernán: D. XIII, 415 (Spinosa, Jean de, B).
Nuñez, Pedro: Article D. XI, 184 (Nonius, Pierre).

SPANISH AND PORTUGUESE WRITERS REFERRED TO 37

Palacios, Miguel de: O.D. I, 7 (N.R.L., March, 1684).
Payva de Andrade, Diego: Article D. II, 79 (Andrada).
Peñafiel Contreras: O.D. I, 618 (N.R.L., Aug. 1686).
Pereira, Gómez: Article D. XI, 546; O.D. I, 7 (N.R.L., March 1684).
Pérez, José: Article D. XI, 564.
Pérez de Montalbán, Juan: O.D. I, 381 (N.R.L., Sept. 1685).
Pineda, Fr. Juan de: O.D. I, 566 (N.R.L., May 1686).
Ponce de la Fuente, Constantino: Article D. XII, 244.
Ponce de León, Gonzalvo: Article D. IX, 168; O.D. III, 609 (Réponse).
Ramírez del Prado, Lorenzo: O.D. III, 365 (Continuation des Pensées diverses, Y).
Ramos del Manzano, Francisco: D. IX, 168 (León, Gonzalès Ponce de, A); O.D. III, 555 (Réponse).
Río, Martín Antonio del: D. XV, 16 (Zahuris); O.D. III, 524 (Réponse).
Rivadeneyra, Pedro de: D. IX, 306 ff (Loyola).
Roca, Conde de la: *see* Vera y Figueroa, Juan Antonio.
Rúa, Pedro: Article D. XII, 644; D. VII, 323 ff (Guevara, C and D).
Sánchez, Francisco: Article D. XIII, 76.
Sánchez, Tomás: Article D. XIII, 76ff.
Sánchez de Arévalo, Rodrigo: D. IV, 565 ff (Castille, Alphonse X de, G and K).
Sandoval, Prudencio: D. IV, 478 (Carranza, C); V, 63 ff (Charles-Quint); O.D. I, 31 (letter to older brother, Nov. 23, 1674), 618 (N.R.L., Aug. 1686); III, 62 ff (Pensées diverses); Emile Gigas, *Choix de la Corresp. inéd. de P. Bayle*, p. 81 (letter to J. Basnage, Nov. 17, 1674).
Santos, João dos: O.D. I, 402 (N.R.L., Oct. 1685).
Serrano, Jerónimo: D. XIII, 413 (Spinosa, Jean de).
Soropán de Rieros, Juan: D. XIII, 415 (Spinosa, Jean de, B).
Suárez, Francisco: O.D. I, 668 (N.R.L., Oct. 1686); Emile Gigas, *Choix de la Corresp. inéd. de P. Bayle*, p. 112.
Tamayo de Vargas, Tomás: D. X, 258 ff (Mariana); O.D. IV, 723 (letter to M. Rou, Feb. 21, 1696).
Teixeira, José: Article D. XIV, 87.
Ulloa, Alfonso: D. V, 63 (Charles-Quint).
Urquiola y Elorriaga, Juan Bautista: D. IX, 168 (León, Gonzalès Ponce de).
Valdés, Alfonso de: *see* Valdés, Juan de.
Valdés, Diego: Article D. XIV, 310.
Valdés, Juan de: Article D. XIV, 306 (includes works by Alfonso de Valdés).
Valera, Diego de: D. XI, 323 (Padilla, Marie de, C).
Vázquez, Gabriel: O. D. I, 668 (N.R.L., Oct. 1686); III, 409 (Continuation des Pensées diverses).
Vega, Garcilaso de la (El Inca): O.D. I, 295 (N.R.L., May 1685).
Vega Carpio, Felix Lope de: O.D. I, 759 (N.R.L., Feb. 1687); III, 202 (Continuation des Pensées diverses).
Vera y Figueroa, Juan Antonio, Conde de la Roca: D. IV, 478 (Carranza, C); V, 76 (Charles-Quint, S); XI, 325 (Padilla, Jean de); O.D. III, 62 (Pensées diverses).
Villareal, Manuel Fernández de: *see* Fernández de Villareal.
Villena, Enrique de: D. XIV, 412 (Villéna, Marquisat de, C).
Vitrián, Juan: D. XI, 33 (Naples, Alphonse 1er de, I).

Vives, Luis: D. V, 61 (Changy, Pierre de); IX, 31 (Lambert, B); IX, 177 ff (Léontium).

Appendix II
TRANSLATIONS OF HISPANIC WORKS MENTIONED BY BAYLE

Translations of works by the following Spanish and Portuguese authors are listed in the *Dictionnaire* and in the *Oeuvres diverses*. The translations are given as listed by Bayle, whether or not they are complete. Where possible, I have checked them against R. Foulché-Delbosc, "Bibliographie Hispano-française," in *Bibliographie Hispanique,* 2nd part, 1912-14 (referred to as Foulché) and Antonio Palau y Dulcet, *Manual del librero Hispanoamericano,* 1st ed., Barcelona, 1923-26, and 2nd ed., Barcelona, 1948-55 (referred to as Palau 1 and Palau 2, respectively). Other references are given in full.

Andrés, Juan, *Confusión de la secta mahometana:* Fr. trans. *Confusion de la Secte de Mahumed,* by Guy le Fèvre de la Boderie, based on the Italian trans., Paris, chez Martin le Jeune, 1574, in 8°. (D. II, 86). Foulché, 399.

Celestina: Latin trans. *Pornoboscodidascalus,* by Caspar Barthius; Fr. trans. by Jacques de Lavardin du Plessis-Bourrot (O.D. I, 757). Palau 1, V, 130.

Cervantes, Miguel de, *Novelas ejemplares:* Fr. trans. by d'Audiguier (D. II, 521). Foulché 943, 997, etc.

Cieza de León, Pedro, *Crónica:* It. trans. by Augustin de Gravaliz, ed. of Rome, 1555; ed. of Venice, appresso Domenico de' Farri ad instante di M. Andrea Arrivabene, MDLVI (D. IX, 168). Palau 1, II, 199.

García, Dr. Carlos, *Antipatia de los franceses y españoles:* It. trans. *Antipatia de Francesi e Spagnouli,* by Clodio Vilopoggio, Venice, 1637 (O.D. III, 521). Palau 2, VI, 56.

González de Mendoza, Juan, *Historia de las cosas más notables.... del gran Reino de la China:* Fr. trans. *Histoire de la Chine,* by Luc de la Porte, Paris, 1689 (D. X, 406). Palau 1, III, 377.

Gracián, Baltasar, *Oráculo manual:* Fr. trans. *l'Homme de Cour,* by le Sieur Amelot de la Houssaie, Paris, chez la Veuve Martin et Jean Boudot, 1684 (O.D. I, 97). Palau 2, VI, 336.

Guevara, Antonio, *Epístolas familiares:* Fr. trans. *Epîtres dorées,* by Guterry, Anvers, 1591 (D. XI, 327). Palau 2, 450.

————, *Reloj de príncipes:* Fr. trans. *l'Horloge des Princes,* by R. B. de Grise, depuis revue et corrigé par N. de Herberay, seigneur des Essars, ed. de Lyon par Benoît Rigaud, 1592, in 12° (D. VII, 326-27). Palau 2, VI, 446; It. trans. by Mambrin Roseus, 1548, another by Fausto da Longiano, 1546, in 8° (D. VII, 323 and 327). Palau 2, VI, 444; Latin trans. by J. Wankelius, eds. of 1601, 1606, 1611, 1615, 1624, and 1664 (D. VII, 323). Palau 2, VI, 447.

―――――, *Aviso de privados y doctrina de cortesanos*: Fr. trans. *Réveille-matin des Courtisans*, by Alexandre [sic] Hardi, 2nd. ed., Paris, 1623, in 8° (D. VII, 326). Palau 2, VI, 452.

―――――, *De los inventores del marear*: Fr. trans. by Du Pinet (D. VII, 326).

Huarte de San Juan, Juan, *Examen de ingenios para las ciencias*: Fr. trans. *Anacrise ou parfait jugement et examen des esprits propres et nés aux sciences....*, by Gabriel Chappuis, ed. de Rouen, 1588, in 12°, another Fr. trans. by François Savinien d'Alquie, Amsterdam, chez Jean de Raveslein, 1672 (D. VIII, 293). Palau 2, VI, 658; It. trans. by Camillo Camilli, ed. de Venise, Presso Aldo, 1590, in 8° (D. VIII, 292). Palau 2, VI, 658, Latin trans. by Aeschacio Maiore, 1622, in 8° (D. VIII, 293). Palau 2, VI, 659 says that this translation is cited but he has never seen it.

Jaramillo, Antonio Matías, *Apologia pro Veritate*: Latin trans. by Pierre Cant, Anvers, 1698 (D. II, 157). Palau 2, VII, 155.

Monardes, Nicolás, *De las drogas de las Indias*: Fr. trans. by Antoine Colin; It. trans. by Annibal Brigantus; Latin trans. by Clusius; English translator unknown (D. X, 486-87). Palau 1, V, 211.

―――――, *De varios secretos y experiencias de medicina*: Latin trans. by Clusius (D. X, 486). Palau 1, V, 211.

Pérez de Montalbán, Juan, *Para todos*: Fr. trans. *La Semaine de Montalban, ou les Mariages mal assortis*, contenus en 8 nouvelles tirées du Paratodos du même auteur. Traduites de l'Espagnol par XX. Suivant la copie imprimée à Paris, 1685. 2 vols. in 12° et se trouve à Amsterdam chez Wolfgang (O.D. I, 381) Foulché, 1885.

Santos, João dos, *Ethiopia oriental*: Fr. trans. *Histoire de l'Ethiopie Orientale*, composée en Portugais par le R. Père Jean dos Santos, Religieux de l'Ordre de S. Dominique, et traduite en Français par le R. P. D. Gaetan-Charpy, Maconnois; Clerc Regulier Theatin. A Paris, chez André Cramoisy, rue de la Harpe, 1684, in 12° (O.D. I, 402). Aubrey F. G. Bell, *Portuguese Bibliography* (1922), p. 347.

Texera, José: Bayle merely says that one of his works was translated from Castilian to French by Dralymont (Jean de Montlyard). He is probably referring to the *Miroir de la procedure de Philippe, roy de Castille*, Paris, 1595 (D. XIV, 88-89). Palau 1, VII, 17.

Valdés, Alfonso, *Diálogo de Mercurio y Carón*: Fr. translator unknown; It. trans. *Due Dialoghi l'uno de Mercurio e Caronte: nel quale, oltre molte cose belle, graziose e di buona dottrina, si raconta quel che accade nella guerra dopo l'anno MDXXI. L'altro di Lattanzio e di uno archidiacano, nel quale puntalmente si trattano le cose avventute in Roma nell' ano MDXXVII. Di Spagnuolo in Italiano con molta accuratezza, e tradotti e revisti. In Vinegia, con grazia e privilegio per anni dieci* (D. XIV, 309). Palau 1, VII, 95.

Valdés, Juan de, *Ciento y diez consideraciones divinas*: Fr. trans. *Cent et dix considerations divines*, by Claude de Kéquifinen, ed. de Lyon, in 8°, par Charles Pesnot, 1563, ed. de Paris, par Mathurin Prevost, 1565; It. trans., Bâle, 1550, in 8°; Eng. trans., Oxford, 1638, in 4° (D. XIV, 308). Palau 1, VII, 97.

Vives, Luis, *De institutione feminae Christianae*: Fr. trans. by Antoine Tiron,

1579 (D. IX, 179). Palau 1, VII 215; another, *De l'Institution de la femme chrétienne, tant en son enfance que mariage et viduité; aussi de l'office du mari*, by Pierre de Changy (D.V, 61). Palau 1, VII, 214.

[Author unknown]: Fr. trans. *Histoire de la Conquête de la Floride par les Espagnols sous Ferdinand de Soto: écrite en Portugais par un gentilhomme de la Ville d'Elvas, et traduit en Français par. M. D. C. (de la Guette de Citri)*. A Paris, chez Denis Thierri, rue S. Jacques, 1685 (O.D. I, 295).

www.ingramcontent.com/pod-product-compliance
Lightning Source LLC
Chambersburg PA
CBHW021848220426
43663CB00005B/453